hazelnut coffee
in a pencil skirt

*Sophia,
you have such a sweet spirit!
keep being you.
you are enough.
— Jodie*

hazelnut coffee
in a pencil skirt

jordan danielle

Charleston, SC
www.PalmettoPublishing.com

Hazelnut Coffee in a Pencil Skirt

Copyright © 2021 by Jordan Danielle

Library of Congress Control Number: 2019935220

Cover Artist: Ashley Smith Heinrich
Instagram: @smith.and.i

All rights reserved

No portion of this book may be reproduced,
stored in a retrieval system, or transmitted in any form
by any means–electronic, mechanical, photocopy,
recording, or other–except for brief quotations
in printed reviews, without prior permission
of the author.

First Edition

Paperback ISBN: 978-1-63837-764-1
eBook ISBN: 978-1-63837-765-8

acquaintance 1
growth 47

Hazelnut Coffee in a Pencil Skirt

…is my testimony. these written experiences are split into two parts: *acquaintance and growth*. from the young teenager that wrote some of these poems to the young adult who is growing and figuring out life. how I dealt with troubles. joy. hurt. decisions. confusion. love. fear. spiritual life change. poetry listened when I thought no one else could. this may come as a shock to those who figured they may have known all of me. it includes various situations in my life that compelled me to write. this is not all of me. just a few things that fit hazelnut coffee in a pencil skirt.

Jordan Danielle

when you step into your purpose.
you don't know what you are getting yourself into.

begin.

acquaintance

HAZELNUT COFFEE IN A PENCIL SKIRT

my joy comes from seeing
others succeed
it comes from happiness
and knowing what life means.
enjoying the ups
and receiving help with the downs
the need to listen and learn
and be involved with the world around.
I know that the truth will
set you and me free
yet it is sad that I
cannot freely be me.
I want to express what
I feel. think. and pray.
keeping the hope that I'll
inspire folks one day.
I know the tongue can
burn and hurt like fire
but I wish I could use mine
for good- to spark as electric wire.
my joy comes from living and learning
and having dreams.
joy is something that I'm
glad God can bring.

December 4, 2010

b a c k w a r d s   c u r s e

some days I wear sweaters when it's hot
because they're comfortable when I'm not
something is very wrong
I cry but want to be strong

July 6, 2011

afraid to love.

scared to experience that feeling.
the feeling when I know that I'm falling for someone falling for his smile. his eyes. his respectfulness and the way he treats me based on the feelings he has towards me.
I'm scared of not being able to wait
until the next time he texts me
receiving joy from hearing my phone ring and seeing his name
pop up on the screen.
nervous about being too excited to see him. even when the last time I saw him
was earlier that day. scared of thinking of him during the day
afraid to wonder if he is thinking of me
and I'm anxious about that text that comes from him during the day that
confirms that he was thinking of me.
I'm fearful of being by his side.
holding his hand. being in public with each other. and getting to know his friends.
scared of being comfortable with him. scared of meeting his parents. scared of meeting his siblings.
scared of preparation and feelings about the dates that we have.
afraid of having those butterflies in my stomach right before
his lips touch mine.

fearful of him walking me to my door making sure I got in safe
scared of having those feelings so deep
that I can't stop from smiling all of the time.
scared of all those things because
I am terrified of …
fearful of…
afraid of…
love.
being so in love and then face the possibility of it being a loss.

the joy that I once had when I saw his name pop up on the screen is now
gone because his number is no longer in my phone. that same smile.
those same eyes. are only memories of the hatred that spilled through that same mouth
that used to curve into the most beautiful smile. those eyes hiding all the lies and deceit.
the same way that I thought about him during the day is now painful
and those texts I used to get from him is now from my friend telling me
about this other girl he is talking to now. the same excitement that I used to get when I saw him
is now painfully awkward when I see him. the conversations
that I would love to have with his parents are now cut short. so short that they

don't exist anymore and I am embarrassed to be seen by them.
anxious.
apprehensive.
afraid.
of losing something that I once had.
afraid of losing something that I have never had.
afraid of never having it.
afraid to love.

b r o n z e

your reaction disappointed me
I didn't know how it would be
but I just knew I didn't want it like that.
smiling? awkward silence. there you sat
you sat there speechless
I sat there. self-esteem gone more less
how did you feel? what was going on
I'm sitting in the dark. humming a song.
acting like everything is okay
like your reaction didn't ruin my day
could it have been more reactive?
I feel silly even suggesting this
who am I to question your response?
but in a contest, you'd only win bronze

February 8, 2012

I am beautiful.

I hate that society says
we're not beautiful unless
we've got light skin, long hair
and wear nothing larger than a size 4 dress.
beauty is much more than that
there are girls and women trying to change
and wishing they were born that perfect way
trying to perfect what is already perfected.
why listen to what others say?
while we are out worrying and fretting
trying to buy that long hair, weave, bleach,
clothes- end up debiting.
why not first look in the mirror
and love who we are.
not everyone has the body of those girls
in a video. dancing with men and cars.
you know what?
even beauty is in the eye of the beholder
that is the beauty of romance
that should make us stand tall and be bolder.
we are never going to be
beautiful in our own eyes
if we listen to movies. videos. or society
most of that is corrupting image into lies
so love who you are…
I am beautiful. this is who I am.

August 1, 2011

JORDAN DANIELLE

on people you can't depend
if so, that's your end.
for you must know
nobody else's flow
but your own.

September 17, 2011

HAZELNUT COFFEE IN A PENCIL SKIRT

act that way you would
not the way they say you should
carefully make the choices you want
be bold and simple like a point.

September 11, 2011

u n d e r c o v e r

sometimes I wish my glasses
would just shield
my expressions and
not reveal
the cruel truth
hiding underneath
the cute smile
showing all teeth
the act gets old
I need to show
my true crazy self
and just glow?
sometimes I wish my glasses
would just hide
the churning emotions
that I feel inside

July 4, 2011

HAZELNUT COFFEE IN A PENCIL SKIRT

keep your pearls
this isn't a game
because when we lose them
behind it, there is no fame.
what would compel us to do
the desires we bashfully wish
he says, "baby let's do it" and we
willingly serve ourselves on a dish.
because we didn't want to wait
until true love found its way
we just gave it to him and now he is gone.
with a piece of us. our hurt here to stay

— s e x

JORDAN DANIELLE

I'm not going to be
that girl you want me to be
I'm not that person
I'm only going to be me.

I'm no replica of who you are.

October 23, 2011

HAZELNUT COFFEE IN A PENCIL SKIRT

he gave me his number
and placed it in my phone
then he smiled all the while
knowing the act was phony.
all he wanted to see was
my gold and precious pearls
but from me he saw none
he can get it from other girls.
why did he choose me?
I carry myself differently.
so guys would know
I'm not the one. they must behave.
I didn't expect for it to be him
he seemed so smart and innocent
yet he wasn't.
I am hurt that I was
played that way- dumbfounded
I just *knew* he was a good one
not just some random dude I'd rebounded.
but for that. he will look again
because I'm gone. bye bye buddy!
I'm sure there are other girls that
would love to get dirty and muddy…
with you.

December 17, 2011

if I were to leave this world today
what would you say about me?
you wouldn't know everything
just stuff on the surface you could see.
I would say I was never perfect
everyone has their flaws
but mine always seemed so big
although I hadn't broken a law.
life never seemed fair to me
I always wanted power to rule it
not everyone's life- just mine
but I'm learning to just relax and sit
if I died today I want to be remembered
even if life didn't work out for me
it is always a special thing to cherish
I've seen things some can't even see.
so I praise God first and foremost
for life itself and always giving us choices.
if I were to leave this world today
it wouldn't matter what you would say about me
I don't care how you judge me
because it is and always is what God sees.

—understanding another day isn't promised

September 18, 2010

in my mind.

we can't say we never tried
to hide feelings and be friends
but we know we can't hide
even after all the amends.
we arrive out of the shadows
and say what's on our minds
now my feelings are coming back
but go. I want my sun to shine.
I've been thinking about this
it's time to let go
forget you
but my mind says no.
it hurts to know
we are far apart
physically and mentally
but I must move on
you can't be my forever
I'll never really forget you
in my mind we'll be together.

not a waste but worth the chase.

you know when you want something really bad
so you try and give all that you had...
then find out what you wanted wasn't for you
yet you worked so hard trying to gain something new...
well sometimes what that was was only a test
working you very hard so you get nothing but the best
instead of getting upset because you think that was a waste
later you will be praising God cause your gain was worth the chase.

October 21, 2011

o v e r n i g h t

I am honestly confused
you say you like me. don't want to lose
the best thing you ever had
yet it doesn't seem like you need me that bad.
we haven't been together for long
and the 'relationship' has never been strong
swore you loved me and would kill if we broke up
but maybe that I will.
honestly, you scare me with that
don't know if that comment is a fact
so I try and hold on longer
maybe this will make me stronger
but for you… I just don't know
if I can take it or just let go.
right now, I am confused
and I really don't want to sound so rude
but you better treat me right
or imma be gone overnight.

November 1, 2011

Yes. I'm upset now
because I realize I made a mistake
my hurt hardened my heart
like warm waters turn to ice on a lake.
I was caring about
what and how things looked like
instead of how things actually were
and how they felt right.
you took me seriously. I made your day
I was on your mind. I even made you smile
but for me you just made me wonder
why I was still with you- in denial
I offer an apology to you
for acting like everything was okay
and not doing or speaking on
what my soul told me to say.
I offer you an apology
because I didn't know what I needed
but now I do and unfortunately

…it's not you.

HAZELNUT COFFEE IN A PENCIL SKIRT

I wish I could be happy
and bubble over like   f
                              i
                                z
                                  z.

foreign to me.

who are you
what is this?
to be treating me the way I should be
why aren't you asking to chill
texting me "wyd"
having your hands roam as your eyes engulf me?
I've never encountered anyone so calm, relaxed and open
someone who I can talk to for hours
and not feel as if it's a game I'm closed in.
buying me lunch. walking me home.
showing up at my work opening doors. being respectful. insightful.
and still a flirt.
introducing me to yourself one part at a time.
you. your friends. family. that's all cool. all fine.
taking things a step at a time. taking it slow.
making sure to stop and give me a hug even if you're on the go
who are you?
a special someone who shows up other guys who don't even had an ounce of the something you have.
a gentleman
what is this?
a friendship that is special. respectful. beautiful. likeable.
a friendship that is growing.
but who are you
what is this?
these actions and behaviors are so foreign to me.

mixed emotions
yea, I feel that
I wish we could be honest and true
this is when I say "it's me not you"
to be honest... I haven't been
I am playing around with folks emotions
not realizing it until epiphany happened then
when I was overwhelmed by the commotions.
I think I want to be your girl
but I need to know if you want me the same
because I will let go of the others. I say no name

—exclusively

nervous.

our eyes meet
your words so sweet
but you're still ...
maybe because you were never made to
and now you don't know what to do.
funny how you sit up with me
until the morning
talking about us. how we met and
building up trust
how can we be laid up watching tv
cuddling. smiling. because we are borderline
fondling our feelings
about one another wondering
if we are for each other.
our eyes meet
your words so sweet
but you're still…
I know you. comfortable with you. and you're still…
discovering more and more about our pasts
seeing what habits left and those that lasted
talents that make both of us see each other
in a different way
than what we believed.
the chance we took when we made plans to chill
and hold each other's hands. the chance to get out
of our comfort zones
and how it led us both to your home
but you're still…
nervous.

how are you still nervous?
what are you nervous about?
when did you stir up this doubt about a simple thing
when did you give me that much power to stay in your mind for all these hours that
you couldn't do something like this... couldn't give me a simple
kiss.
nervous.
day four. you close the door
you turn off the light and prepare yourself
your eyes look me over and
I can tell you need no help
a jump or literal leap onto me where your body lies against mine
a lapse of minutes. seconds. there is no time.
just physical silence. yet we're having conversation.
a single lick of your lips was your demonstration
a smirk from me because I had been waiting all this time
for you to get the courage to have your lips
meet mine.
sweetness. softness. sexiness.
nervousness – gone
heartbeat racing.

f*boy

I am upset because I shouldn't have.
shouldn't have broken my barrier
and let you in
I shouldn't have responded to you
shouldn't have smiled back
when you had that goofy grin
I shouldn't have waved back when you asked
why I was going out
because you were used to me staying in.
I shouldn't have associated myself with them
because they associate with you
I shouldn't have said yes
when you asked if I wanted to come over
I shouldn't have invited you to my celebration
I shouldn't have been at your place on a day
so special to me
I shouldn't have been at your place so many times
I shouldn't have gotten
to know your friends
I shouldn't have spent the night at your place
I shouldn't have trusted you
I shouldn't have believed that you were actually different.
I should have just stuck with what
I thought of you
before I knew you.

good for the night.

bring them out at night that's where the love
is the best
don't bother showing affection in the day to
all the rest
hide your feelings. your wants.
desires. keep your pride.
don't fall too short. in fact, so short
that you can't see how tall
when you can't see how tall, how are you
to know how hard you are going to fall?
good for the night.
show the beautiful cool colors of togetherness
to all who are awake
only good for the night
the other vibrant colors of the day
have to wait.
who do you show the events of the night to
when will you share the feelings of night to the day
when will you share you?
good for the night
well that's not good enough
for me.

solitude.

being alone
alone: without anyone or anything else
alone is being by myself
how can I be lonely?
lonely: without companions; solitary
I am surrounded by people.
they are all around me like a
swarm of bees surrounding honey but all I want is
solitude. I want to be alone. I want to be lonely.
but I can't
I cannot be without anything else
because I find myself alone with me.
alone with my thoughts
alone with my ideas. perceptions.
and debates in my head
never fully alone when I have you to contribute to
my thoughts.
thinking of what you are doing
how you are feeling. if you are stressed
and how you're dressed. if you are laughing and
smiling enjoying your time
if you are in the café waiting for food in line
my thoughts are simply about you.
my ideas are ones that some may categorize as crazy
and too soon
my ideas of the possibilities of us.
the idea that we could be more than a situationship
yes, more than that- a relationship.
I can commit to you and me

I can commit because I am never lonely.
alone with my thoughts
alone with my ideas
my hopes of ...us
alone with the distraction of thinking ahead
alone with the distraction of thinking ahead
alone with the distraction of thinking ahead
alone?
I want to be alone
I want to be lonely
I have to be without anyone or anything else
I have to be without you.

solitude.

the decision.

I was the one
we were the one
he was the one
we all figured it would be best.
it's the age
it's the different paths
it's about our places in our lives…
but what about our talks
the way we listen to the requests of the other
the way we can both talk to each other about Him
how we can live for Him
what about the way we hold each other accountable
the way we feel a connection with each other
care for each other…
time.
time is not our friend
but we can be?
it's not fair how I can love seeing you
want to be with you
but then we're only friends because of time.
how does time have the authority
to tell us what we should do
how we should feel about each other
how can time make me put these emotions I had for you on hold?
to make time do what is always does
it still goes on…

HAZELNUT COFFEE IN A PENCIL SKIRT

I seem to be in the same uncomfortable spot
where I was when we made that decision.
that decision to let time
make the decision
for us.

the one I dressed for.

you.
you are the reason why I struggled picking out
what to wear the first-time meeting ya
how surprisingly difficult it was to throw on clothes
to impress you
like maybe if I dress up. look nice. my personality
might interest you
or in your case… my body
you.
you had the ability to create these flying creatures
inside my stomach
when I first saw you
from not knowing who you were. to wanting to know.
and getting to know...you.
and in a week's span of time the same you who I got
to know somewhat and be cool with
isn't the same *you*
in fact. it's like the you I was so worried about
impressing
transformed into a product
of whatever else is depressing.
the *you* I am familiar with now would have
discouraged me
from getting to know you then
communication.
had you communicated who you are- your intentions
then I could have made my decision based on me
yet *you* showed me the you that you knew I'd like
the you that *you* had to learn. observe. and create

the you that had me stressing over what to wear
whether I'd be covered yet cute or
liberal and sexy
you showed me the *me* you wanted wasn't
the one I dressed for.

rant.

I'd rather you tell me
I'd rather you keep it straight
tell me what you think this is
tell me what you want it to be

don't leave me wondering what you really want.

rant part II.

you need to man up
boss up
and play a better hand when you are
dealing with me.

it ruins.

I want to tell you how
much it hurts.
I want you to understand why I act the way I do
think the way I do
it's because I have been played a time or two.
the deceit of guys not worth my time
tears because I gave them mine, but sadly
I was renting a slot on the schedule I shared with other girls
I wasn't exclusively his. not the only girl in his world.
I want to show you how much it hurts.
how embarrassing it is.
I want you to feel the way I felt.
so I carry those feelings
into the next encounter showing
I carry that hurt. confusion and anger
and I don't give the next guy the benefit of the doubt
it ruins.
it's so easy to be a player when no one is pushing you to become
something better.
it's so easy that's why we
aren't together
it ruins.
I want you to know how much it hurts.

what are "friends" like.

friends can be like
food and water
use it when you need it
if so they're not friends
friends can be like celebrities
you look up to them
for fashion. advice
ideas and looks
friends can be like
big champion boxers
getting fame and fortune
for knocking people down
friends can be like a diary
keeping secrets and will
always be there
when you open up
what are all friends like?
I don't know
I just listed a few
that I knew.

rant part III.

sometimes you give advice
you don't use yourself
thinking you are high and mighty
and that you don't need any help
you will think that
for only so long
until someone else comes around
and very much proves you wrong
I assure you that person
wasn't the one you would've expected
to come and correct you
not one you highly respected
but at least you got in line
now you know what's up
hopefully that person was just enough…

October 22, 2011

this feeling.

I believe I am a wonderful actress
there is nothing wrong
yet there are tears on my mattress
from the strange feelings of wanting you
cause when I had you I didn't want you …now I do
it is crazy how this episode even played out
we said things when
we didn't know what we were about
so that's why were in this hazy space
and our thoughts and feelings have no real place
to be set aside and thought through
our actions carefully judged too
all I know is this feeling is alien to me
because it has been some time since
I let my mind free

where do tears come from
heartache. pain. sorrow
the knowledge of the fact
you don't know how to get through tomorrow

where do tears come from
confusion. loneliness. anger
the need to come up for air
but somehow holding on to the anchor

afraid of how things will unfold
will it be mean. kind. bittersweet?
needing a good distraction
will you open up to lyrics and a beat?

where do tears come from
it's the emotions all bundled up
trying to burst like fireworks
from a beating heart shaped cup

December 4, 2010

rant part IV.

I hate that I empathize
I hate that when I care
about someone I hurt for them
their pains I bear.

I hate that I care so damn much
why do I have to feel.
when does anyone care so much
about me. who prays for me to heal?

I prefer it to be dark silent
in order for me to hear my own cries
know that it's really me feeling the way I do.
empty. confused. hurt. and a little lonely too
I prefer it to be like the present state my
feelings towards you are…

— d a r k   s i l e n t

current relationship status.

coffee shops give me joy
when I walk in they hug me
with the sweet and bitter smell
of coffee
and greet me with the writings on
the wall
the people stare at me like they don't
even notice my existence
and my coffee enters me like
it's been waiting for me to
need it

when the sun rises and when the moon glows.

when the sun rises
I feel free
like bursts of energy
running through my veins
trying to play this game called life
can be difficult I'll say
but you must learn the rules
that's what everyone yearns
to know the rules is very bright
there are tools in every light

when the moon glows
I know
that everything will come to a close
things that happened will stay in
and everything broken will mend
freely this is my alone time
to sit and think-
when the sun rises and the moon glows…
I know it is all mine.

December 5, 2008

truth is
love is a four-letter word that I used to be afraid of.
as a child I thought it was necessary.
that it was something
that went in between I and you too.
and it came so naturally that I
believed that love was something easy.
that love was what makes us happy.
but then I avoid love.
so instead of getting close to it I decided to cheat it.
I would take all the benefits of the relationship.
but you can keep the feelings part.
I wanted to escape the assumed hold on love
and save the hurt of my heart.
truth is
after all the hurt. pain. confusion.
issues of self-esteem. lacking love.
rejection of there ever being a possibility of love…
my heart still hurts and the mess I'm in
led me to You.

growth

people's perception of you is not entirely your fault
why give their perceptions power over your identity.
who are you if no one thinks twice of you
who are you if you are not identified
by your own doing?

continue the race ahead of me.

Lord, there have been times I thought I'd quit the race.
the race ahead of me
retreat and not have faith.
I was caught up in the now. I was anxious because I wanted things to change yet I didn't know how.
I didn't know how things could get better.
I didn't know how things could get right.
I wanted to drown myself in my problem.
depress and cry myself to sleep every night.
I didn't care that there were those there who encouraged me along the way
to read the Word. to trust and obey.
I figured that retreating. backing down from the race was the best way to go
that shows you how much I know...
I tried my way and of course stayed in brokenness.
no way could heal my wounds and
get me out of my mess. no way but *the* way. the *only* way. Jesus.
if I take advantage of the gift of life that He so freely gives. He could be mine and I could be His.
if I confess that I tried other ways to heal
yet stayed in brokenness...
if I would believe in my heart that Jesus sacrificed His life so I can be set free
from sin that I would be saved from hell and have Holy Spirit within.
if I would trust and give my life to the one who gave His own...

when I have my mess. trials and tribulations
I won't be alone.
oh how He loves me.
oh how He loves me.
How He loves me so. so much that
He chose me before I chose Him. so much that He
gave His life for our sin and before
we chose Him back then. the love He has for us to
not leave us deserted. for us
to abide in Him. lean on Him when we are hurting.
that's the type of love
that no one else can provide
It comes from the Ones who look low but sit high.
I am thankful for those times I thought about quitting
the times I thought about throwing in the towel
and receive all the hell I was getting.
it made me understand the power of God's love to
send his only Son
from above to take our place on the cross
to save me.
to save the lost.
those times made me stronger in my walk. it made
me grateful for Jesus
and made me want to live for him for a number of
reasons
because He first loved me.
therefore, I will keep the faith
and continue the race ahead of me.

twenty years is enough time
to see the world for what it is
but not old enough to know
what to do with it

— e x p e r i e n c e

confidence.

respect yourself.
if he calls you
you don't have to drop everything
and answer to him
because when time comes will those guys do the same
as you do for them?
you lose your respect when you put that guy
before others
who have proven their worth to you plenty of times.
when you run to accommodate him
you don't know
how many times he spits game to different women
perfecting his lying rhymes but here you are
putting him first
tricking yourself into thinking you are putting yourself first
getting what you want, what you deserve.
but at what cost?
what's the price?
you're not confident in yourself that if you
miss a call it's possible to return it.
if you spend time with your family
instead of him
another day will come and it won't hurt a bit.
but what you are doing is putting him first
despite what's going on
and that shows the level of confidence in him
to treat you as you treat him

and from that you should already know where he belongs.
he deserves a seat on the outside of your circle
to be invited in on your time in order for you to make time for those
who have already proven their worth to you.
instead, you may gain a doozy
spend all your time to figure out that's who he is
you lose him
and the ones that really matter too.

the truth doesn't hurt me. it keeps me alive
because my mind and my body are numb
immune to each and every lie. I'm paralyzed
the truth wouldn't hurt it would help
my limbs move some

first date inquiry.

it's going well
the going is good
I read. I pray. I act as I should
my life has changed. I'm living for God
I don't do the things I used to because
my life is a living thank you.
for Christ enduring the cross. dying. resurrecting. for me and you
so that we may have salvation
and we can spread the good news.
so we could make the decision on what life we choose
whether we live for Him or live for the world
and that is where I begin today. are you living for the world?
have you given your life to Christ?
I need to know these answers before I even think about how you look nice.
I want to know if you are
firm in your belief
that you take it seriously
I need to know because when I date. I'm not dating for just now
I'm dating for the future
if we become engaged somehow.
I'm thinking long term
because this time is an investment
this time isn't time to be messed with. I don't need to know about how good

you are in bed or what lustful things are inside your
head.
I need to know that you care about me, that you
respect my decision to follow
the One and Holy
my decision to choose Him instead of this world
so that's what you ought to think about when you
choose this girl.
I am a child of the one true King
and that means more than the world
it means everything.
so before there is ever an us
I must ask you...
have you given your life to
Jesus?

when I hear your name
my soul stirs.
like cream swirling in black coffee
beautiful swirls that are endless
like the end of time.
and You are the cream
that no matter how long the swirls
last the black coffee will sink
and you end up on top.

—JESUS

instead of looking for the right someone we want
let's take time to become who we intend to find
because once we found who we were looking for
will we be ready for them or ready to break them?

with my eyes closed.

saturday mornings.
slow and steady without regard to
what is happening outside this room
opening of my eyes awakening from a dream
expecting to see you laying on the other side.
only a visual. a dream of my innermost desires that
we can't quite tell each other yet.
you aren't here but the sun is
it's shining and its rays invading my facade
the curtain I put up to refrain the sun from invading
to shield the outside to keep my saturday morning
slow and steady.
moving. trying to adjust in the circumstance that
happens to be my bed.
I close my eyes trying to imagine
you were here again
I can't even see your face.
anxiety hits me. no it's my hand that tries to shield
the invading rays
from the sun interrupting my views awakening me
from my innermost desires.
it is the reason my eyes opened. the reason
I couldn't see you
the reason why you're not here. a tear escapes from
my eyes I shoo it away
but understand it's because I have to close my eyes
to see you with me.
I have to close my eyes to see you across from me
smiling

just because I was there.
closed eyes imagining us laughing on the couch because the universe
saw fit to provide us with an opportunity such as this to witness the
connection how we actually click.
with closed eyes you are my best friend, my companion when my eyes are closed
I am what you need. I am serving you.
showing my love to you
I am cooking for you. helping you pick out what to wear. making plans with you
I am supporting you
I am with you.
with my eyes closed I was in your arms smiling because you were with me.
you were making plans for me
you were here.
with my eyes closed
but the sun interrupted my views and brought me back to reality
the fact that you're not even here
and you don't even know.

time
is something that will
always
tell on itself.

— l i f e

someone else instead of yourself.

it's here. it's time to confront what I once stated
being afraid, terrified of love
and all that people make it
it's time to confront because it's here. it's arrived
all the built bonds. trust. friendship. laughter has contributed to
all the feelings that I have inside
now another fear has crept in and it's the feeling of uncertainty.
the way that you treat me. speak to me. act with me. makes me wonder
if your feelings have arrived for me
I can't imagine being afraid of something yet confronting what I have no control over
I must control what I do. what I say. maybe stay away and battle with
being sober. I just want the same. I want to be on the same page
yet there may be a possibility that you're not on the same page
or even the same chapter
or even the same book
but I just wish that is what's coming soon because I can see in the future
the white dress. the family. the petals. the plane and the honeymoon.
but I'm nervous
afraid
terrified

of it being in reverse.
instead of us it's you and another lucky woman and I get the invitation and on the
day of I go over the lines that I've rehearsed "I'm so happy for you"
"have a great life" but inside I'm dying ...
holding back the anger, the hurt and the sobs I have inside
I couldn't take it if that were to happen
I would be smiling on the outside while you were walking down the isle
with your wife.
everybody clapping...
it's here. I don't know what hurt would be worse
the hurt of the idea of possibly being in love and losing it
or the idea of being in love
staying in love
and watch the friend you love
love someone else instead of yourself.

HAZELNUT COFFEE IN A PENCIL SKIRT

you told me I'm one of two or three people
you could have a real conversation with
and instead of taking the compliment
I wondered who the other two people were.

shouldn't envy. patience is a virtue
envy is sin and patience requires trust
these are the things that us humans lack
it describes the hurt in all of us

flesh loves the flesh.

I flirted with the dude and laughed at his jokes. I even gave him my number
then I told my girls. I told them about this cute dude but instead of praises and 'ooh girl'
they brought up You.
I want to say I thought about You. I want to say I did.
but his focus was on me and my attention was his.
he asked me out on a date and that was just fine
except that he wasn't Yours, yet You were mine
but we conversed anyhow and the flesh loved the flesh.
we enjoyed each other's company and forgot about the rest.
after that we were in his car talking. laughing but then he took it too far
of course he didn't know he was taking it too far
because he didn't know that he was Yours and You were mine
because the flesh loved the flesh and we forgot about the rest.
he leaned over and his lips were the perfect set of temptation
but I thought about the months of hard work and dedication
that I put into You- that I put into us.
yet there I was with the sin of lust.
I was going to cheat on You.

—When Jesus is 'BAE' (before anyone else)

"if you were real
why is there a huge hole
in the sweater you knit.
I hear them say that it was knit
just like you, in the image of your
own.
I can't imagine your sweater being as holey
as mine.
If you were real, how could I suffer
like I do.
it's not like I chose my sweater
from a rack.
if I could, I'd go- no run
and take this shit back.
if you were real
why couldn't you overcome
who they call the ruler of the air?
he has taken a hold of me
and I can't seem to see
who you are and how you are
real?
make me feel like you are real.
give me a sign.
there must be some confirmation
if I conform
and act like the other sweaters,
to try and hide my hole.
but it's too big.
if you're real.
stitch this hole

and make me whole
oh Holy One."

—an empathetic perspective of a gay man at bible study

JORDAN DANIELLE

I hate that I gave
any guy
so much power
in my life.

But growth.

cheating.

I thought about cheating today
just picking up the piece
and throwing it away
but then I changed my mind.
I just wanted to take this knife
and stab it in my heart
the pain wouldn't compare-
even taking my life.
what if I cheated today
who would say anything anyway
finally, I'd be alone
but the pain would have won.

when your heart sinks isn't that the most
beautiful pain. it's like you feel the ache
it's not just mental. the sinking gives you an
estimate of how much hope was at stake.

this is supposed to be her safe spot
everything she says here is confidential
so when she says she doesn't like living anymore
does confidential still sound reasonable?

I am okay with feeling.

I used to run from you
because I thought I knew your type
I labeled you one way and somehow you
didn't end up that way.
you ended up better.
so I started running more.
hiding. not speaking to you.
not going to the same events as you.
I ran. because that's what I do best.
I run and avoid things that would make me feel.
too much experience told me that if I didn't run
you would interest me. we would talk. you would excite me
we would see more of each other. happiness.
then you would excite me less
because my detective skills would find some reason to distract me.
we would see less of each other. conversations dry and less of them.
then one day there would be none.
so that's why I run.
because I would feel. and I couldn't take that risk
with your type. but you're not your type, are you?
you're better.
so I run. because I'm afraid that you would interest me.
pursue me. excite me. engage with me. happiness.
reach goals with me. worship with me. and not leave.
I run because I am confused about what happiness
with a man

looks like. Am I ready to be happy? to accept great?
I used to run from you. but now
like the introvert I am… I am fueled by aloneness with myself
but nowadays I get another spark to fuel me when I see you.
when I see your love for Christ. when I see your servant heart.
I still run.
but this time to you.
and this time I am okay with feeling.

warm like my coffee
when it sits for awhile
like the expression of what
I feel for you in the curve of my smile.

warm like the sun
baking the light onto my skin
is how I feel when you have
me all jittery and fuzzy within.

screenshot.

it captures the intense moments
that I want to cherish for awhile
the silent wishes. hopeful thinking
that is expressed in the curve of your smile
while you stroke your pen across the page
express your deepest thoughts
wants and desires
who you want to be
who you want to be with
how you will build
who you will inspire…
it captures what my mind longs to see
day to day
wondering if that's what you see when you
scribble on that page…
it captures the intense moments
and holds it in a bottle
so if I do forget…
it will remind me tomorrow.

you left me in the most vulnerable spot
if I needed to escape before, I ran to you
but if I need to escape now
who can I run to?
we used to lurk in the shadows. live in the dangerous half-truths
breaking rules that weren't even set for us yet
we were the reason the rules were created.
knowing that we dare not love yet we were infatuated...
with each other.
if I was lonely all I had to do was think of you and you would already be on your way.
you used to be my safe spot. I could tell you things that I could not tell anyone else
you knew every part of me.
you knew me to the point where I thought no one else could know
I was comfortable in the fact that only one person truly knew who I was
yet you were a mystery to me.
we held conversations in silence and
listened to what each other needed without saying a word
you always knew what I needed. you always knew what it was.
I tried to get insight on you but couldn't because
you were there for me. it pleased you that you pleased me
it didn't matter that you wanted something more than what we had
as long as you had something.

you put the decisions in my hands knowing that I would fail
you knew that you wanted to love but I wouldn't let it prevail.
I didn't know that you left a spot for me
I had no clue that you were hurting this time
I thought we were just two messed up people
trying to fill voids in our lives and add some too
so imagine my surprise when you left my place
turned around came back and said "I love you".
you left me in the most vulnerable spot.
not because I didn't feel something towards you too
it was just I was afraid to love you and you'd run out
and if I needed to escape with someone who could I find
who knew me as well as you
who knew how messed up I was
yet could still utter the words that seeped from his heart as you did?
you knew me so well so it didn't surprise you that I used college to run away from us.
that I knew 3 hours' worth of driving to and from would be too many miles on the car you
lease that I was physically escaping you but I should still call you at least?
not even a call or a text because what we had was toxic.
I would literally do anything for you that wasn't honest.
2 years later I see your face
you stop me and look at me the way you used to.

you frown and say I changed.
I smile and say good.
it's been a change you can't even imagine.

—when the past pays a visit

"weird"

weird because no longer is there a conformity amongst social standards.
yet a refusal or incongruity of the 'plus one'
brought to the party. weird because once akin to the values shared
once congruent to the business declared.
the business.
booming.
the products dispersed throughout the country, the state, the city the town,
my school, my friends. the business broke even with the investments
and profited because the product is being sold better than ever.
the product of normality
uniformity
mediocrity.
the product shapes the market. it sells for cheap and everyone is buying
social standards brand the product calls it 'new' 'exciting' but we all know
that they are lying.
weird because that product is being sold.
once a consumer, now a reviewer.
negative vibes where the reviews were once high because the product is the
injustice to freedom. the chains of consciousness. the anchor of transition.

weird because instead of continuing to use
the product that set the social standards
that had little to no depth entailed, the standards that were impossible
for every consumer to meet and be satisfied...
but I knew the greatest gift available to all
that showed me resistance to conformity lessened mediocrity.
weird because I see it as a gift, a favor. they see it as a loss. an endanger
to the standards that had them comfortable in normality but couldn't see
that what I had was better in actuality. I was given the gift of the Holy Spirit.
the grace of God. the forgiveness of sins by the blood of Jesus, the love of God
through faith. I could not possibly go back to the sellers of the world because I'm
sold out to Christ.
weird because I'm no longer a consumer. I'm comforted in God's love and I've found my
identity and it's not in the product sold. it is in God because He is the one who accepts
me and calls for me to be bold.
bold in the truth
bold in the gospel
weird because I'm a representative of Christ
and it shows from the fruitfulness
of my life.

HAZELNUT COFFEE IN A PENCIL SKIRT

brown is not the color you ought to fear
black is not the color you should try to avoid
yellow should not be the reason you want to mix black and white
and white doesn't mean racist

JORDAN DANIELLE

I'm not your friend
if I'm your black friend.

—you're not my white friend

HAZELNUT COFFEE IN A PENCIL SKIRT

beauty was still beauty when we were eleven
like when sprouted leaves turn colors
they are beautiful until they fall off the tree
and they turn into the color of dirt they were left in

"because at first I saw her
and she wasn't like any other girl
that I have had before.
a different look.
then, I heard her
and she didn't speak like any other girl
that I have had before.
then, I followed her
and she didn't go to the same places
as any other girl that I have had before.
I kept following her.
and it lead me to the front of the Church's door.
I saw her praises, her serving, her friends
and I understood.
it made me question.
if my relationship with God was good …"

—"unequally yoked"

so gone rap challenge 2017

success
who is the one to arrange the limit we can reach.
reach out and be the change.
validation of our individual names.
create the truth and get rid of all the claims
but who is telling us?
who is teaching us? it comes from the youth
it's then when they craft the truth.
they said the world is ours it's what we make
it but what about those who heard that truth
and didn't take it.
the crafted truth. the one we feed our youth.
chewed by society
digested to our brains. withheld from our soul
bowl movement of our culture which
explains- how we got our names.
but what if I told you the world isn't yours
and I go against what
you were taught before. see it's not yours
it belongs to God. your temporary reside
is all you've got.
so our truth can't remain the same
we've got choices to be able to change.
question: do we let the world define our
success or do we give it to our Creator and let
him finish the rest?
I mean we are here for a very short time so
who cares of the wants of
yours and mine. the world is His

he is the one to arrange
the limit we can reach and our life after this
he is the one
who breaks our hearts with love for Him and
make us a new creature.
born again.
so the truth is we need purpose in our lives.
the world may think we are strange but
success is in the end when
God validates our name.

release.

why is this your prime
you pick a little off of
me and make it yours
invite it in and make it mine.

how can you watch me succeed
and not wonder how through
everything I'm not broken. not broken
not in pieces. can you believe?

where have your morals gone
when did you stop living by what you
used to and expect me to still be
where you have ceased. I've gone.

it is so hard to be patient when others have
when others are happily thriving
and I'm secluded. involved in a relationship
that I was told would revive me

metaphorically speaking.

the hole is what they call it
when you disobey their orders
and your actions don't meet their approval.
you're thrown in with the hopes of reflection
they deprive you of what they feed you
and leave you to your own devices.
darkness surrounds you and they hope
that it consumes and drives you.
drives you away from sanity and back
into their arms
where you would look to them for the answers
for the solution to the problem.

you forgot how to think for yourself.

pretty foolish to look to them who threw you in
with hopes of you learning your lesson of
how it feels to go against them.
so next time they throw you into the hole
because there will be another time…
I pray that you aren't afraid to open your eyes
you aren't afraid to feel and keep the hope
not in them but the spirit inside of you.

January 18, 2017

singleness is a gift from God and marriage is too.
it's just all so differently thought out since
we've been dreaming of marriage
since our youth.
defining what we would later classify love as.
as if he didn't have all of these qualities then
he wasn't meant for me.
it started with fairy tales and playhouses.
he has to be a prince in shining armor
and when I tell him to come rescue me
he has to come fighting
each
and
every
obstacle.
and it is then, at the end
once he proves my worth to him
we live
happily ever after.

—false reality

HAZELNUT COFFEE IN A PENCIL SKIRT

they're just three words
when he says them it is not the peak
in your relationship they are just words
until his actions correlate with what he speaks.

you've never given me a reason to be
jealous.
never given me a reason to think that I'm
sharing.
your being always affirmed
I am the only one.

wonder how.

I stared at the wind today
I was still and observant.
I stared at the wind and tried to understand.
I imagined that I was the wind and
I felt that that was too much responsibility.
too much strength to go against the normal stillness of the atmosphere
I stared at the wind today and observed
the audacity it had
to interrupt the still nature
and cause a rift within it.
I stared at the wind today and wondered how it became confident
confident enough to have other objects in its path follow in the direction it blew
I wondered how it became so loud
a whoosh displaying the strength, audacity and confidence the wind has within it
I stared at the wind and I wanted to be it.
I wanted to be unpredictable in the measures of my strength.
no one knows when the wind will blow slightly or rush deeply
yet the impact remains.
I stared at the wind today and
got excited by the way it made me feel.
a cool sensation and my skin reacted
I wanted to be the wind.

I stared at the wind wondering how it could be so strong
I wondered who orchestrated the movements of the wind to interrupt the normality of a situation
to be strong in it and
show its strength in different measures
to allow feelings to arise that weren't there before.
I wondered how the wind could do so much and it was... just the wind.
I stared at the wind today
and decided to swallow it.
I am the wind
and no longer do I have to wonder how.

why am I the hope?

I am broken more so than anyone else
there is a struggle every day to turn from the world
that I am used to and to follow Christ.
there is nothing that I do to make myself worthy of
the hope you have in me.
don't put your hope in me
that is too much pressure
don't tell me that I'm the only one you see
as fruits of your labor
that's too much pressure.
I don't labor and follow Christ
for your hope to be in me
obedience from me comes from the love and trust I
have in God
not from your hope in me
don't position me as your hope
don't tell me that I am your hope
because I've been someone's hope before
the one that has done something right who they
could brag on to their friends
and say "look what she has done"
I've been the one that people say "oh I've heard so
much about you"
"you're doing so well oh you're doing so good"
I've been the hope.
and when I'm the hope it sucks.
because those who have their hope in me are
satisfied.
don't put your hope in me. I don't do this for you.

JORDAN DANIELLE

don't tell me your hope is in me because
if I wasn't rooted in Christ
I would stop all the good that I do
and I'd do what I want to.
then that will show you
who your hope ought to be in.

the river washes away the scent of you
so I can forget what you smell like
what if I drown myself in a river of tears
will it wash the memory of you away?

I remember you were the one back in the day
who inspired me to write a poem.
to inspire them to be about you.
you were the one that made me notice you
you came to me smiling and said your name
and you held your hand out for me to shake
I, in turn, told you my name
we were to be friends later on
despite the difference in classification of grades.
we would be friends with something in common
it was there in that theater room where I would
realize that things happen for a reason.
after that day I would run into you 3 times before
we would meet again in that theater room.
conversations were always started by you
there was always something to talk about
I was rarely alone with you on the other
side of me waiting for our scenes and critiquing
the ones ahead of us
you were always there. it was like you were taunting
me. like you knew that I would fall for you and that
you just were waiting for it to happen.
you were there to get me out of class
to walk me to the car where my mother waited
for you to come to her smiling and say your name
and for you to hold out your hand for her to shake and
in turn for her to say her name.
charming.
now she won't forget about you and she won't let
me either.
you were always there.

in the neighborhood. in my classes. on stage. on my phone. in the pages of my poetry.
you were the one who led me to believe.
who led me behind the stage... behind the curtain.
you were the one who let it slip.
who knew what guilt was when you brought her to the show.
where was she the whole time?
I still remember you like back in the day.
because my mother still asks if you work
where you do. like I keep tabs on you...
because when I open the pages of poetry I still
see you and because my best friend sent me a video of your proposal.
you're getting married.
I am so happy for you.

I wasn't good with goodbyes
didn't like saying it. didn't like ending
something that I didn't want to end
now goodbyes are needed and don't faze me

HAZELNUT COFFEE IN A PENCIL SKIRT

rip my heart open and keep living
go on and keep cutting it open
distress my heart like a pair of jeans
hanging in the store window they're sold in

my soul has been shaken
by storms that you
have never seen me
go through.
so don't tell me I'm too old
to cry. don't judge me when a tear
escapes from my face.
it's my soul's response to the reoccurring ache.
the ache that you now contribute to
and if I didn't love you so damn much
this would be the last day
that we would ever keep in touch.

—reoccurring ache

HAZELNUT COFFEE IN A PENCIL SKIRT

do I look like I am a blank page
waiting to be filled in by you
like I have nothing to offer to this story
and I need you…?

him: hey, are you good?
me: yea I'm just fine

I just want to know what is running
through your mind
you must think that I need you…

him: so what do you think?

about what

me: I mean that's cool

I hope I didn't just give you
the answer that you wanted
I'm too tired to care…

him: we can still be friends

no. we can't still be friends
I don't need you around anymore
him: Jordan?
me: yes?
him: are you listening? we can still be-
me: friends? I think not

I am good on my own. I was fine before you.
do you think I need you?

him: why? look we have come this far together
me: what is that supposed to mean?
him: it means that we shouldn't part just because-
me: because we aren't together?
him: right.

ha all this time I thought you
were trying to save me.
trying to fill me. when all along
you needed me

me: I think it's best if we make a clean break
him: but Jordan-
him: I just-
me: don't want me to be your girlfriend but your friend
him: right.
me: goodbye

unique reaction.

for many responses not worth my time
they acquire most of my energy
when I require energy for things
and people of importance
where does the energy of my response go?
is it hidden in the surprise of the depth of
dedication.
maybe squandered on things
that create happiness
for such a small part of time.
but where is my unique reaction to You
the One who requires the highest energy
of praise
of adoration
of glory
the One who has created me to create the energy
and the desire
to praise Him for simply who He is.
where does my energy go?
what hinders me from producing that unique reaction
to something so sovereign that it decimates everything
that gets sin the way of His will.
where is my energy going?
why have I given it precedence over Him
in my life?

a ship sailing with no captain.

it seems as if you are happy then
you will be happy when
yet that is not the whole truth
those lies remain most uncouth
as a people we are content until
accepting the fulfillment of will
we think we have got it in our hands
though its further away in its own lands
we propose that he or she is the one
but we never know until it's done
we want it to come about that way
the feeling now, not going. here to stay
that belief is never going to happen
like a ship sailing with no captain
even if it seems that you're happy then
you might not be happy when…

January 21, 2012

spring now, all flowers- no thieves.

like gold is ready
I knew this day was coming
fixing what goes down. plumbing
it's easier to say
that bad was then yet brighter is today.
the connection between bee and honey
ours is so real unquestionable almost funny
the change that occurred, metamorphosis
enjoyed having time to look back at this
summer was then blooming was flowers
having peace and joy we called ours
autumn was then beautiful leaves
yet spring is now all flowers no thieves
can't steal my joy and happiness

JORDAN DANIELLE

she clung to me
as if she needed me
she consulted with me
before she made a move
and honestly it was quite annoying
but I had to look deeper than that.
she clung to me because she needed me.
and I listened to her presence.

—hurting but healing

HAZELNUT COFFEE IN A PENCIL SKIRT

it's crazy that now love has found me
I have yet to write.
it's like I'm too busy being in love
to record it all.
too busy. too busy.

—getting back to myself

it's funny how far
love will go
to test how much you
really want it.

credit.

just like you give photo creds to
whom
it is due.

who are you
giving credit to
when folk
look at you?

lunar eclipse.

I waited
for you
to invest
in me.

little did I know
you already were.
we just needed to meet.

this morning.

I woke up this morning
and all at once your flaws
that I hid from heart
emerged.

it was overwhelming like it
was too much and the levy broke
my heart to follow suit.
doubt.

your words sound like what
I've been needing to hear
what I've yearned to know but waiting.
action.

you seem to have a plan making
making them and adding me but what about you
your spiritual goals striving to…
stagnant.

your purpose.

eighty hours
is enough explanation
it says all that you won't
except it doesn't.

forty-eight hundred minutes
whispers the faint reason
that this is all coincidence-
merely happenstance.

two hundred and eighty thousand seconds
yells to me that within each one
you are focused on it
driven by it.

HAZELNUT COFFEE IN A PENCIL SKIRT

I often say I write when I feel something.
I felt a lot this year.
but until now no poem has been written
no pen to page.

too much to write.
because if I write it
it means it's real.

JORDAN DANIELLE

there are patches in my memory
from the gift of forgetting
rather than forgiving.
because how can I be hurting
from something that didn't happen?

sometimes I look at other authors.
I feel their poems.
they make me love
make me mad
make me curious
they make me feel.

I wish mine would do that for others.

self-doubt is a disease that spreads
from one thought to another.

don't get sick boo.

I lost 35 pounds
healthy habits. self-love. discipline.
and the weight slowly shed.

the weight wasn't the only thing I lost.

they see you doing well.
and wonder how it's happening for you.
how you were just with them.
in the same position.
but now you've moved higher.
fake smiles, fake happiness for you.
they wonder how.
you don't even notice.

watch them.

HAZELNUT COFFEE IN A PENCIL SKIRT

I cut the sugar
from my daily coffee.
and I lost
a few pounds.

it was holding me back
from my potential.

I cut a few things
and people
from my life.

I watched myself flourish.

You thought you could stop my shine.
You thought I needed you to succeed.
You thought I wasn't smart enough to see right through you.
You thought I wasn't strong enough to say no.
You thought no one would stay to watch me shine.
You thought I would believe that I wasn't capable of shining.

Girl, you obviously need to rethink.

my heart breaks when I put so much effort
into someone
something
just to have that thing or person hurt me.

my heart must
keep breaking
keep beating
keep believing

I've hurt others.
hurting can't be the worst.
it's a reminder that we are human
we hurt sometimes.

JORDAN DANIELLE

he got one more time
to call my
natural hair
"frizzy"

it's not worth it.

—your values, dignity, and respect

JORDAN DANIELLE

I'm stuck in between giving up
and going harder
because failure keeps happening
but it can't be the end.
work gets put in and
the results may vary
but the work can't stop
and the failure can't stop
because what good is it
if I'm good at it all?

—am I built for this?

I've failed many times.
I will continue to fail.

But Lord, you never will.

JORDAN DANIELLE

every day
on my way to work
I am reminded of
the privileges some children have over others.

the large homes that line the street
to get to that school
where one semester of tuition costs more
than a full year at my university.

every day when I leave work
I remember the kids I see
every Wednesday
while volunteering at that public school.

how those kids don't differ much
from the kids at the private school.
same dreams and aspirations
same inquisitive interests in the world.

same grade. different teachers
same grade. different resources
same grade. different support
same age. different experiences.

these students speak of
going on trips out of the country.
birthday trips to New York at age 8
meanwhile this bilingual child doesn't know her own birthdate
never seen. only heard of the place of her family origin.

every time I go to work
I am reminded
of the innocent privilege these seven and eight-year
old's are afforded
that other seven and eight-year-old children

not too far away
haven't seen and couldn't imagine.

all of us
putting effort into
you
won't help
unless
you
want to help
yourself.

HAZELNUT COFFEE IN A PENCIL SKIRT

I expect so much
from myself

that it becomes too much
and I can't win.

tough love
has me up
all night
praying for you.

we're both hurting.

HAZELNUT COFFEE IN A PENCIL SKIRT

I'm glad

        nothing is

                revealed

                        all at once.

we all experience
twenty-two
differently.

relax.

HAZELNUT COFFEE IN A PENCIL SKIRT

when you told me I couldn't
I did.
just to show you
I could.

I lost myself;
and my purpose
within it all.

—second thoughts

JORDAN DANIELLE

I will never forget
the woman
I talked to
who had her life planned
nice paying career
corporate lawyer.
and left it all
because she valued her children
her family
more than business.

HAZELNUT COFFEE IN A PENCIL SKIRT

connections
are
needed.
don't be afraid
to put yourself
out
there.

—me, everyday

JORDAN DANIELLE

I'm having second
and third
and fourth
thoughts
about
this.

HAZELNUT COFFEE IN A PENCIL SKIRT

my eyes are red
not because there
were tears
but because there were none.
empty stares
in the middle of the night
till the crack of dawn.

my alarm signals time to get up
but my eyes have yet to rest.

JORDAN DANIELLE

it's becoming harder
and harder
to trust people
it's easier to be alone.

—the trap

HAZELNUT COFFEE IN A PENCIL SKIRT

loneliness
is comforting
making conversation
with others
is tiring.

so I rest a lot.

JORDAN DANIELLE

still learning
how to accept
and give
love.

HAZELNUT COFFEE IN A PENCIL SKIRT

when these walls adjust
their age yells present
when life calls the roll.
life was there when the walls were fairly new.
waiting for a loving family to make memories inside them.
the walls could only listen to the years
fly by
they couldn't tell of the lives they held
when these walls adjust and settle. it's an exhale
a constant reminder that whether that loving family
was still together or not
life goes on.

JORDAN DANIELLE

I refuse
to be limited.

because I serve a God
who is limitless.

HAZELNUT COFFEE IN A PENCIL SKIRT

is it gratifying?
when you
tear down others
who are working
on their craft
just because they have
less experience
than you?

nah fam, let's build each other up.

anger.
because
I am learning
how to
feel
more emotions.

HAZELNUT COFFEE IN A PENCIL SKIRT

this past week was a blur
I don't remember much.
I just know how I felt all week.
confused and angry.

—me, at disciple group one week

JORDAN DANIELLE

I am reminded of God's
grace and forgiveness
and I'm learning to give
it to others.

HAZELNUT COFFEE IN A PENCIL SKIRT

it's okay
for you
to be happy
for others.
without comparing
yourself
to them.

JORDAN DANIELLE

why is it that I'd
rather dance freely
in a sea of people
dim lights. loud music
a drink in hand
than with a few people
lights on
my face easily recognized?

—Saturday nights.

HAZELNUT COFFEE IN A PENCIL SKIRT

you're hurting
yourself
too much
being upset
because you see
that I'm
finally
                      happy.

JORDAN DANIELLE

you're the same
toxic person
and I'm still hoping
that you'd change.

I'll change instead.

rant part V.

I'm not going to make you
feel comfortable
When you're around me
by feeding into your perception of me
if you look at me and still see the girl
I used to be
it seems proper to remind you

that I'm growing.

out of character.

superb actors.
we played the characters
until we became them
lost ourselves.
found under a new name
except we forgot that eventually
we'd have to exit stage left
and realize that our souls
had nothing left
too consumed in this character
though the play is unclear
the identity is fear
and I understand now
why I'm out of character.

as unrecognizable as my pain.

it seems like a forgotten tale. an unrecognized hardship.
something that didn't need attention brought to it.
rarely was it that I wrote about the really hard stuff.
the stuff that made me hard. made me cold. bitter.
relentless against all of the good that life would offer
I made it my task to bear the pain.
I bore it well.
I bore it so well that no one could tell that I was on the brink of letting the façade go.
so well that even I started believing that I was alright.
that I could bear this pain alone. it wasn't pain that I was bearing
it was secrets.
are those not the same thing?

I am unraveling.

I know what I feel is pain.

I understand that I need help.

maybe one day when I heal. every time I write about it

my tears won't make the words as unrecognizable as my pain.

trying to describe my feelings after breakup.

it's like I dropped an item
and it landed in the crevices
between the couch and back wall.
and instead of moving the couch
to allow myself
to reach the item
I squeezed my arm through
reaching. looking. searching
for that thing that I dropped.

for awhile I feel stuck
lose all feeling in my arm
still steady searching
until finally-
finally the couch is moved
just a bit
and my arm is released.

no need for tears.
just relief.

insight.

vision is so much clearer through the pain
it's like those rose-colored glasses melted onto my face
scalded my eyes
you brought forth new vision
vision that in that past relationship
that I thought would take me to the altar
there were so many things that I should have taken to the altar
to give to God and let my wants go
sometimes the pain creeps in and disguises as numb
sometimes it takes 9 months
to birth a breakup poem
vision is so much clearer
through pain
unreconcilable pain. pain undiscussed
vision that exposed the holes in my friendships
that exposed my need for Jesus.
because I have Him
I have more than enough
eyes set on the Lord
life aligned to glorify Him,
grace given. mercy overflowed
prayers never ceased
and under all of that pain
in spite of all that pain
His vision is released.

JORDAN DANIELLE

I listen to the birds chirping.
while the winds are howling
they fall silent during the storm
just as I do
thunder and lightening
left to do its work
and I will survey the destruction in the morning
… every morning.

they came in the middle of the night
during the day
to steal your peace
interrupted your esteem
and how you spoke with me
wrecked havoc in your kitchen
the place you prepare your nourishment
fed you lies
as if you weren't heaven sent
these thieves stole your couch
right from your living room
so you had no comfort
in your place so you figured
you'd leave soon
they ransacked your bedroom
looking for your love and security
clothes thrown. mattress lifted
exposing the impurities.
these thieves came in the middle of the night
during the day
even while you're home
stole it all from up under you
and made you wish you were alone.

—insecurities

in the next five months.

be more kind to self
drink your water
mind what is yours
care for your health
walk in your purpose
don't doubt the Lord
be grace filled with self
learn to accept help
forgive yourself for your past
tell shame and guilt you're
breaking up with them- it can't last.
give more and learn balance
no longer is your writing a hidden talent
stay in therapy and work towards healing
so you can be available for clients and their feelings
stay in church and be involved
going beyond the hours within the church walls
research and save resources to go towards a house
love the Lord and self in order to love your spouse
completion of these things by said date isn't necessary
but progressively the nature of these things will be
primary rather than secondary
I write these as goals to live by
because in the next five months you'll be

twenty five

2021

somebody's therapist. *

my journal's name was Zarea.

How crazy is it
that a child personifies
the pages where she stores her innermost
dreams. desires. and feelings.

How crazy is it
that she only desired for Zarea to listen
she didn't have expectations of Zarea
other than to be there
and allow for her to have a space
where she could feel appreciated. loved
allow her to have a space
where she could be herself.

How crazy is it
that this teenager understood
that she didn't have the space she desired
so, she created one.

How crazy is it
that this teenager realized
that not only was this space just for her
but she was speaking to others
unbeknownst to self.

How crazy is it
that despite
the plans that that teenager had of being an attorney

the plans that that teenager had of defending. or supporting others
there came a divine redirection. a realization that others can use their voice.
teenagers can speak up for self. individuals can seek their sense of self.
couples and families can communicate. express their needs to get to healing.
they need a space to feel welcomed. listened to. seen. heard. healed.
one that is theirs and a professional who cares.

So, to the teenager who personified her journal
called it her best friend
because she was lonely…
no longer will that teenager, now adult
keep those feelings inside
and feel that there is no other way to share
No longer.

But how crazy is it
that the teenager is now publishing a few. not all. of her poems
and that teenager, now adult
is somebody's therapist.*

Sometimes redirection is necessary.
to be obedient to God's plan and to walk
in my calling and purpose.

2021
*Marriage and Family Therapist Intern, clinically active & in supervision.

HAZELNUT COFFEE IN A PENCIL SKIRT

sometimes the most
dangerous things
are the most heartfelt
and caring
and normal
things you can do in life

—selflessness.

to my Husband.

as I re-read some of my poems from years ago
preparing to publish
tears escaped from my eyes.
it started with one warm, salty liquid
sliding its way down from eyelid to my chin
but then its friends decided to join and before
too long, a few of them were sliding down my face
like its own stream
and music seeped from my mouth
sounding like a painful scream.
and then laughter accompanied it… because how could it not?

how believable is my story?
my testimony from not knowing myself
becoming acquainted with life and trying to figure it out.
thinking I am not deserving of love. afraid of it. unsure of what it looks like.
and then, finally, to surrender my life to Jesus and learn to love myself.
go through hard situations. mature. learn. grow.
and for God to order our steps
for us to finally *see* each other
after having our paths cross more than a few times
we were finally able to meet.
so sweet to look at you
and see the epitome of my desires and dreams of what love looks like.

it is true and within you.
to end this poetic journey
with the recognition of who I am. whose I am. having
Christ at the center of my life
it makes perfect sense to end this part of growth with
marriage.

"I vow in front of family and friends to choose you
daily. To love you unconditionally
and to stay in our covenant forever. I love you."

2021

JORDAN DANIELLE

one flesh in Holy Matrimony
with Christ leading our lives
    a three-strand cord is not easily broken.

remembrance.

naked. I come to you Lord
baring all that my clothes try to conceal
I come this way God to show you I trust
you with my life. my hurt. sorrow.
Lord, I trust you to heal…
I surrender what I have tried to hold on to
I give it all to you.
I surrender all to you when everything is going right
I make sure that it's not my will to be done
not my name that is glorified
not me who can take credit for the things that are
going right
I surrender all to you because you deserve it
you deserve the glory
you deserve the honor
the praise
and glory
and God I'm going to give it to you
I can't forget the times when I didn't
want to be bothered with anything
that had to do with you
when I knew of you
but rejected the truth
I lived the opposite
of what you would have for me
but it was your love that brought me back
changed my heart. my desires. and set me free
God now when I think it's too hard for me to go in
when evangelizing just isn't going my way

when friendships don't happen
I'm excluded from x, y, or z
I have you and all that you have done
sharpied into my memory
because I once didn't follow you
I once didn't care
I was struggling with life. hurt. sorrow
and didn't realize throughout all of that
you were there.
but my life…
didn't show it.
I didn't acknowledge your spirit within me
I gave some things to you that were too big for me
and the rest I thought I could handle…
but God before you I stand.
naked.
bearing all that my clothes try to conceal and wouldn't understand
that this is necessary to glorify you
to bring others to experience your love and develop
a relationship with you.
this is a remembrance of what you did for me
so when I am out in the world
doing your work…
Lord, I don't get weary.

poetry was my best friend.
she listened when I thought
no one else could.

Hazelnut Coffee in a Pencil Skirt

God's amazing love, grace and mercy are the reasons why I can share my journey.

THANK YOU

to my amazing husband for literally all the things. support. love. kindness. gentleness. patience. great ideas. for spending the rest of your life with me and showing me a love that literally the girl writing these poems desperately needed but didn't know how to receive.

to my parents for loving and raising me to be the woman I am now. who were always there for me. I credit my strength. resilience of my faith. confidence. care and so much more to my parents. I often hear from others that my parents did a great job with me. I concur. when I told my father that I would be publishing a book, he smiled. he remembered the third grade me who told people that I would be an author and illustrator when I grew up. I thank my mother for facilitating the courage I had to share my art. thankful for her insight and for showing me that I should always trust God with all my endeavors. my parents' support means the world to me.

to my family. my loving grandmothers. grandfathers. aunts. uncles. for loving. supporting. instilling values in me and for encouraging to continue in my faith. to my cousins… y'all are like my siblings. I am so proud of us. we are strong. we can do what we set our minds and hearts to do.

to my best friends. my family- in- love. church family. friends. you all have been amazing. you all know me as me and love me just the same. to my "big sisters". many mentors. professors. classmates. coworkers and others not mentioned. you know who you are.

thank you to my friend & fellow graduate cohort member for the beautiful cover artwork. your time and dedication to capture the essence of these poems onto the cover is amazing.

and finally, thank you to the Palmetto Publishing team for the care in the publication of my collection of poems.

Jordan Danielle